Transferring
Designs

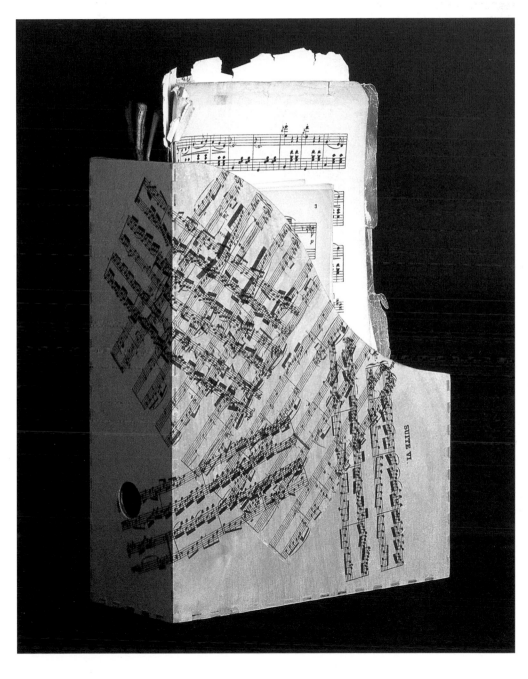

This book is dedicated
to those with
the imagination
to create.

Transferring Designs

SIMON RAW-REES & MICK KELLY

SEARCH PRESS

First published in Great Britain 2002

Search Press Limited
Wellwood, North Farm Road,
Tunbridge Wells, Kent TN2 3DR

Text copyright © Lazertran 2002

Photographs by Charlotte de la Bédoyère,
Search Press Studios

Photographs and design copyright © Search Press Ltd.
2002

ISBN 1 903975 20 4

The Publishers and authors can accept no responsibility
for any consequences arising from the information,
advice or instructions given in this publication.

Publisher's note
All the step-by-step photographs in this book feature
one of the authors, Mick Kelly, demonstrating how to
transfer designs. No models have been used.

If you have difficulty obtaining Lazertran, please write to
Lazertran (UK) Ltd., 8, Alban Square, Aberaeron,
Ceredigion, SA46 0AD; LLC, 650 8th Avenue, New Hyde
Park, NY 11040, USA; e-mail mick@lazertran.com or for
more information visit www.lazertran.com

Printed in Spain by A.G. Elkar S. Coop. 48180 Loiu (Bizkaia)

Acknowledgments
*Many thanks to the designers and artists whose work
appears in this book.*

Page 1
Music file
*Photocopied musical notes have been overlaid on a wooden surface
to create an original decorative file.*

Page 3
Candle magic
*Images can be stamped on to Lazertran paper and transferred on to
candles or any other wax surface. The technique is simple and
extremely effective, and it can be seen on page 38. The stamp design
is reproduced with the permission of Rubber Stampede.*

Opposite
Gilded plate
*Butterfly designs have been transferred on to the back of a glass
plate. The plate has then been gilded to produce a beautiful effect.*

Contents

Introduction

Lazertran is a revolutionary transfer paper that allows any design to be transferred on to a huge variety of surfaces. It is amazingly versatile and easy to use, and breathtaking results can be achieved simply by colour photocopying images on to sheets of Lazertran, which is available in regular or Lazertran Silk.

You may already be familiar with heat set photocopy transfers, but Lazertran is different: it is a waterslide transfer paper. This means that when images have been photocopied on to it, they can be soaked in water so the images slide off as transparent decals. These decals can be applied to almost any surface, including wood, paper, rough or smooth stones, fabric, and much more. Images can even be layered one above the other because the decals are transparent and allow the colours to be seen through each other. Stained glass can also be simulated with beautiful, glowing colours.

Lazertran Silk works by transferring designs with an iron rather than with a decal. The resulting effect is soft to the touch, and unlike other heat transfers does not ruin the 'hand' of the silk. Lazertran Silk can also be applied to various surfaces with spray mount (see page 60).

A favourite of interior designers, Lazertran has been featured in many television programmes in the UK and US. Possible applications for this type of use include murals, decorated floors and furnishings.

Lazertran papers were developed originally for use in art schools, as a way of transferring images on to canvas. The resulting questions about other surfaces meant that further applications came thick and fast: ceramics, glass, metal, stone, fabric, polymer clay and more. Further experiments led to their use for etch resists on metal and glass, and on vacuum forming plastic in product design departments.

We had great success in art schools, both in the UK and US, and the more applications we found, the more crafters everywhere were becoming excited about the possibilities of Lazertran. At the time we were unfamiliar with many of the crafts, but we developed ways of using Lazertan on metal foils, stamping, embossing, glass decorating, memory cards, decoupage, polymer clay and silk.

As support for the art school applications we produced a workshop video which was successful, but did not illustrate the range of uses that would be of interest to crafters. While experimenting and developing the range of Lazertran uses, we discovered that crafters would much prefer a practical book to a video. Search Press saw the excitement around our booth at the HIA craft convention in the US and at many other trade fairs, and for the first time decided to publish a book about a particular product rather than a generic instruction book on a single craft.

The book is divided into sections, based on the surfaces to be decorated rather than specific crafts, and is illustrated with our pieces, plus work made by leading designers and artists. You will find alternative methods of image transfer under each section, because the papers are versatile and can each be used in a variety of ways. We have tried to make everything as clear as possible. If our instructions are followed we believe that, not only will you have hours of crafting fun, but you will also produce extremely professional results that will extend and enhance your particular craft or interest. You may even be inspired to try some of the other crafts featured in these pages.

Mick Kelly

Simon Raw-Rees

Machine embroidered bag

This detail from a bag was inspired by a sketchbook design drawn by Maggie Grey. She transferred it to cotton fabric using Lazertran and it was then applied to a velvet background with stitching to merge the fabrics. Metallic stitching on water soluble fabric was placed over this to enhance the image.

Materials

You do not need many special materials to transfer images with Lazertran. Most of them can be found around the home, or in most art and craft stores. There are two types of Lazertran and both are amazingly versatile. Images are printed on to the paper using a colour photocopier (see page 10), then they are transferred on to your chosen surface.

Lazertran

A sheet of regular Lazertran is made up of a sturdy backing paper which has a slight bluish-green tinge. On this is a separating layer of adhesive and a very fine, clear film of acrylic on to which the image is printed. This film slides off the backing sheet when it is immersed in water for a minute or so. Once released, the film can be applied to non-porous, smooth or textured surfaces using the adhesive on the back of the film. Regular Lazertran can be used on a multitude of surfaces including all types of paper, wood, ceramics, glass, metal, plastics, fabric, wax, eggs and stone. You can also stamp and emboss on to it, then transfer the stamped image on to challenging surfaces such as wax (see page 56).

Lazertran Silk

This is slightly different from regular Lazertran in that the product does not support a thin acrylic film. The image is transferred using heat from an iron, spray mount adhesive or by direct contact on to polymer clay. Lazertran Silk is used for transferring images and designs on to silk, satin, metal foil and polymer clays.

Surfaces

Throughout this book there are projects and ideas showing you how to transfer images and designs on to any surface. Lamps, lanterns, candles, bowls, trays, tins and boxes are all suitable. Surfaces can be flat, curved, smooth, rough or textured. The beauty of Lazertran is its simplicity of use, and the effects you can achieve with very little effort. Plain objects can be embellished and enhanced to complement your home decor, or to transform them into decorative features for a special setting.

Both types of Lazertran have a wonderful transparent quality which means that the surface supporting the image is visible. This quality can be used to transform designs: backgrounds can be gilded to give a rich, glowing effect, or you can allow the surface texture to shine through and add a richness to the design. Pictures can also be laid one over the other, giving a new direction for decoupage. This technique is particularly effective when it is used over metal leaf and antiqued surfaces.

Photocopiers

Images are transferred on to Lazertran using a colour photocopier, and should be printed on the shiny side of the paper. To save time, make several photocopies of your images and keep them for future projects. Make sure you fill the sheet with images to save paper, or use off-cuts of Lazertran if you want to reproduce stamped images (see page 56). Where images are to be photocopied in reverse, the instruction is included in the projects.

It is worth using a good-quality photocopier if you want the images to reproduce well. Ink-jet machines cannot be used with Lazertran. Many of the black and white and desktop laser printers are insufficiently ventilated so they will become too hot. Canon, Xerox, Minolta and Ricoh all make suitable copiers. It is best to use the large commercial photocopiers found in copy shops.

Keep the transfer papers protected in their packet until you use them. If they are creased or bent, they may jam in the photocopy machine.

Other materials

Absorbent paper for removing excess moisture and glue.

Iron for ironing transfers on cloth or metal foil.

Silicon or non-stick baking parchment to act as a barrier between the iron and your image when you are fixing a Lazertran or Lazertran Silk image. Regular greaseproof paper is unsuitable.

Shallow tray to hold water for soaking and releasing the transfers.

Scissors or sharp blade and metal rule for trimming the photocopied images.

Soft sponge or squeegee for removing any air bubbles. One good idea is to buy a window squeegee, pull out the rubber blade, and cut it into 10cm (4in) lengths ready for use.

Clear acrylic medium to seal the image or design on porous surfaces. An alternative is watered-down craft glue.

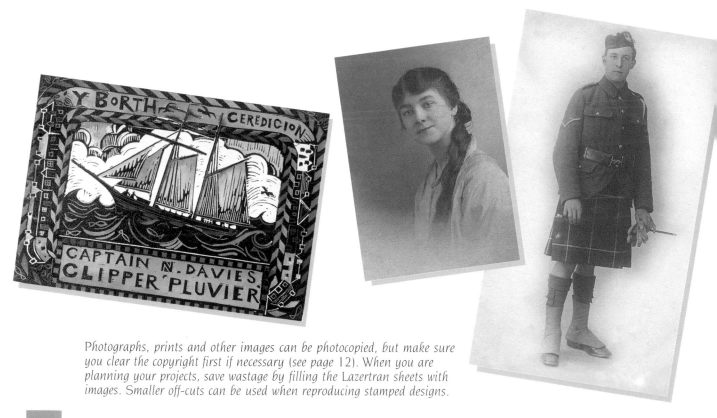

Photographs, prints and other images can be photocopied, but make sure you clear the copyright first if necessary (see page 12). When you are planning your projects, save wastage by filling the Lazertran sheets with images. Smaller off-cuts can be used when reproducing stamped designs.

Short-haired paint roller for applying acrylic glue or mediums.

Spray mount for use with Lazertran Silk.

Turpentine to dissolve Lazertran images into surfaces such as stone and handmade papers.

Paintbrushes for brushing on turpentine, adhesive or acrylic medium.

Cutting mat to protect your work surface.

Wooden board to stretch your paper on.

Varnish to protect the images – both acrylic and oil-based (not shown).

Guide to the materials photograph above:
1. Absorbent paper
2. Turpentine
3. Iron
4. Acrylic medium
5. Spray mount
6. Short-haired roller
7. Squeegee blade
8. Sponge
9. Shallow tray
10. Wooden board
11. Rule
12. Craft knife
13. Cutting mat
14. Scissors
15. Paintbrush
16. Paintbrush
17. Paintbrush
18. Silicone baking parchment
19. Brown gummed tape

Above

Materials used for stamping and embossing (see project on pages 56-57).

Images

You may copy any image you like on to the Lazertran papers if it is for your own use. If you want to sell any of the items you make, or use them in a commercial way, you must clear the copyright of the image first. If you are unsure about how to do this, simply use your own designs, paintings, drawings (not copied from elsewhere) or photographs you have taken. Stunning effects can also be achieved if you photocopy items including leaves, flowers, petals, feathers, shells, scraps of fabric, handmade papers, beads and buttons.

Another alternative is to use copyright-free designs. There are many design books available, which contain a wonderful selection of motifs, patterns and pictures. Computer clip art can also be a good source of images. Old letters and postcards which are out of copyright are another excellent source of interesting images.

Images produced using Lazertran are transparent, so it is best to transfer them on to light-coloured surfaces. Black or dark-coloured backgrounds will make the image more difficult to see, though these can be used to produce interesting and more subtle effects. You can also gild or decorate the surface before transferring the images, to produce interesting effects that show through the transparent decals. After the images have been transferred, they can be worked into and defined using acrylics, oil paints or solvent-based marker pens. The possibilities are endless!

Many different items can be photocopied and used to decorate the various surfaces shown in this book, including leaves, lace, feathers, photographs or buttons. Use them as backgrounds, or overlay images to create unusual designs (see page 58).

Using Lazertran

Lazertran is easy, fast, fun to use, and extremely versatile, covering more craft applications than any other transfer technique. Beautiful, detailed images in glowing colour can be transferred on to almost any surface to create unique effects. There are several ways to transfer the images, using either the adhesive on the back of the paper, acrylic medium or craft adhesive, a hot iron, an ordinary domestic oven or turpentine.

Here we show you how to use Lazertran, but there are a few things you need to learn about this amazing paper before you begin. It can be used to transfer images on to non-porous surfaces: sheet metals, glazed ceramics, glass and plastics, wax, soap, or varnished wood. It can also be used on porous surfaces: paper of all kinds, from thick watercolour paper to fine tissue, canvas, wood, plaster, stone, unglazed ceramics, fabric, shells, walls, floors, ceilings and furniture.

Porous surfaces

In general, porous surfaces need to be primed with acrylic medium if the turpentine method (see page 20) is not being used. There are a few simple rules but the techniques are simple, and they can all be seen on the following pages.

Some surfaces must be prepared first, such as paper, which should be primed with acrylic medium and stretched on a board. If you are using canvas, it is also a good idea to place a flat board underneath, so that the image is transferred on to a firm surface.

Wood and plaster should also be primed. If the surface is curved or contoured, hot air from a hairdryer can be used to mould the image around the curves. If you would like the transfer to sink into your chosen surface, or if it is rough, for example, stone or driftwood, you can 'melt' the image into it with turpentine.

Non-porous surfaces

Non porous surfaces do not need to be primed. In most cases the adhesive on the back of the Lazertran decal will be sufficient to fix any image. Again, the techniques are simple and they are all illustrated in the projects on the following pages.

Fixing and finishing

Images and designs can be protected after they have been transferred on to your chosen surface. This is recommended if the item is functional rather than ornamental. If you are applying images to non-porous surfaces such as glass, tiles or metal, they can be protected with varnish, or they can be baked in a domestic oven to give a more robust finish and the appearance of enamel, glaze or stained glass.

If a more durable finish is required, the adhesive on the back of the transfer should be washed away before the image is applied, face down, on to the surface. If this method is chosen, the image should be photocopied in reverse. The decorated item should be placed in a domestic oven and the temperature should be increased gradually, over a period of about half an hour to three-quarters of an hour, until the transparent film melts (at approximately 180°C (400°F) or gas mark 7). The finish should have a hard, glazed appearance.

If you are using a porous surface such as paper, matt acrylic medium can be applied to give it a matt finish. If you prefer a shiny finish, choose a gloss acrylic medium. Each is applied in the same way using a soft paintbrush.

Above This selection of porous and non-porous surfaces illustrates the versatility of the two types of Lazertran. Images and designs have been transferred on to paper, metal foil, ceramic, wood, fabric, polymer clay and wax. In the case of the candle, the designs were stamped on to Lazertran first, colour photocopied, then transferred on to the wax surface. The techniques are all discussed and illustrated on the following pages.

Facing page Images can be applied to curved or contoured surfaces, like this decorative doll, designed by Robin Schoenfeld around several rubber stamp images from the US-based company Acey Deucy. These were hand stamped on to Lazertran with permanent ink.

Paper

You will need

Regular Lazertran paper
Drawing board
Watercolour paper
Brown gummed tape
Acrylic medium or watered
down craft glue
Scissors
Shallow bowl and warm water
Short-haired paint roller

Both types of Lazertran can be used on to any type of paper, from cardboard through watercolour paper to handmade paper or fine tissue. The regular Lazertran method is shown on these pages; for the Lazertran Silk method see page 60.

A heavyweight watercolour paper was used for the project. As the technique involves moisture, the paper must first be stretched and sealed, then allowed to dry, to prevent it cockling when the image is applied. The image sticks to the paper surface when acrylic medium is used.

1. To stretch the paper, lay it on a flat board and dampen the whole surface with a wet sponge. The paper will expand slightly.

2. Secure each edge carefully with wet gum strip (brown paper tape backed with water soluble adhesive). As the paper dries it becomes taut.

3. When the paper is dry, apply an even coat of acrylic medium over the whole surface using a short-haired roller. Leave it to dry.

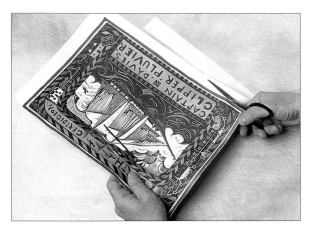

4. Work out where the image will be positioned and lightly mark the area on the watercolour paper. Carefully cut around the picture.

5. Prepare a shallow bowl of clean warm water and immerse the Lazertran with the image facing you. Soak for approximately two minutes.

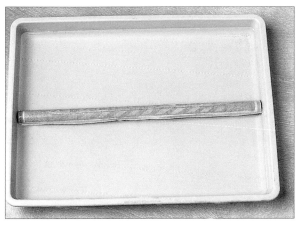

6. The Lazertran paper will curl up in the water. While you wait for this to happen, apply a fresh coat of acrylic medium to the surface of the stretched paper.

7. Carefully remove the Lazertran paper from the water. As you do this it will start to unfurl. Continue pulling it out of the water, then place it on a flat surface.

8. Gently slide the image partly off the backing paper and prepare to lay it on the stretched, primed paper.

9. Lay the image gently on the watercolour paper and position it carefully, sliding out the rest of the backing sheet.

10. Using a roller, gently remove any air bubbles and excess acrylic medium. Leave the image to dry.

Taken from a lino print by Stuart Evans

The finished picture

The paper was allowed to dry, and an even coat of acrylic medium was applied over the whole area. The image looks as if it has been painted on to the watercolour paper. The same effect can be achieved with canvas, or any other absorbent paper surface.

Childhood memories

This design by Robin Schoenfeld was based on an old
black and white photograph of two little girls in a park in
Guatemala. It was blown up to a size of 125 x 125mm
(5 x 5in) and copied on to Lazertran Silk, then ironed
on to 10mm Habutai silk. The silk was layered on to a
small canvas with acrylic medium, and painted with
delicate acrylic washes to tint the image. When it was
dry, torn pieces of decorative rice paper were collaged
around the edges to frame the picture.

Lampshade

As lampshade paper is extremely porous, with a crinkled, rough texture, the real turpentine method is used here. This method has the advantage of dissolving the image down into the paper like a proper print. It would be difficult to apply the transfer to the crinkled paper using acrylic medium, and the finish would be shiny. With turpentine, the transfer takes on the shape of the paper and any shine disappears as it dissolves into the shade.

Make sure you use real turpentine: a substitute will not do. Take care that you read the manufacturer's warning. Protect your hands with gloves, and work in a well-ventilated room.

First, photocopy the image on to regular Lazertran paper, then cut the design to size carefully and soak it in a tray of clean water for approximately two minutes.

You will need

Regular Lazertran paper
Paper lampshade
Small, soft paintbrush
Real turpentine
Tray of water
Absorbent paper

Note: *before you attempt a complex shape like this, practise on a small sheet of paper.*

1. Paint a coat of turpentine over the surface of the lampshade where the image is to be placed.

2. Remove the image from the water tray and blot any excess moisture using absorbent paper.

3. Slide the image a good way off the backing sheet, and position it on the paper by lifting and dropping it in place.

4. Paint the image with a light coat of turpentine, taking care not to over-work it as this will break up the image. Leave the shade to dry overnight. Do not attempt to remove bubbles or creases as the image will have begun to soften. Overnight, it will melt down into the paper and any bubbles should collapse of their own accord. If any bubbles or shiny areas do remain, apply another coat of turpentine to remove them.

Fabric

Closely-woven cotton gives the best results, but many different types of fabric can be used. Regular Lazertran and Lazertran Silk can both be used to transfer images on to fabric. Regular Lazertran is used in the project on these pages.

Regular Lazertran

If the fabric will need to be washed frequently, it is best to use regular Lazertran, which is demonstrated here. As the method involves ironing on, the image should be photocopied in reverse. Make sure you use a silicone paper such as baking parchment paper when you are ironing, as waxed or greaseproof paper will not work.

You will need

Cotton t-shirt
Image
Lazertran paper
Scissors
Non-stick baking parchment
Iron
Sponge

1. Cut out the image you want to use, making sure that there are no white edges, as these will show up on the fabric.

2. Place the image face down on the front of the t-shirt. Use a hot iron and press the back of the image. This will melt the transfer on to the surface of the fabric.

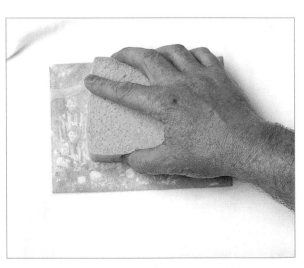

3. Moisten the back of the image with a wet sponge and allow it to soak for two minutes.

4. Peel away the wet backing paper carefully from the image.

5. Wipe away any excess adhesive with a sponge. Leave it to dry completely.

6. Cover the image with baking parchment and iron it carefully on a hot setting to fix it.

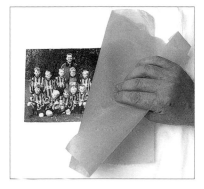

7. Let the parchment paper cool, then peel it off carefully. If the image looks as though it is 'sitting' on the surface, you may need to repeat steps 6-7 to drive it into the fabric well and eliminate shine. Increase the temperature slightly and iron the transfer again until you are happy with the result.

Note

After washing the t-shirt, always use parchment paper to protect the transferred design when you are ironing it.

Original photograph taken by Les Shaw

Silk

The iron-on technique shown here is used with Lazertran Silk to transfer images on to silk or other fine fabric. As with all ironing applications, the image must be printed in reverse. The best fabric is closely-woven, sheer silk such as Habutai. Satin is another ideal surface because of its fine weave. If you want to use fabric with a more open weave, the spray mount method is better than the iron-on method. Lazertran Silk can still be used.

There is no need to cut away any excess paper around the design because Lazertran Silk does not leave a residue on the fabric. Any 'white paper' areas will show only as natural silk on the finished article.

If you are making silk images for greetings cards, follow the step-by-step instructions here, then simply apply the silk image to the card using spray mount.

You will need:

Habutai silk
Lazertran Silk
Iron
Non-stick baking
 parchment
Shallow plastic tray
Warm water
Clean cloth to iron on

1. Place the silk over the image and iron it well until it adheres firmly to the fabric.

2. Immerse the silk and Lazertran, paper side down, in a shallow bowl of clean, warm water, and soak it until the backing sheet falls off.

3. Lift the silk out of the water and lay it face down on a clean cloth.

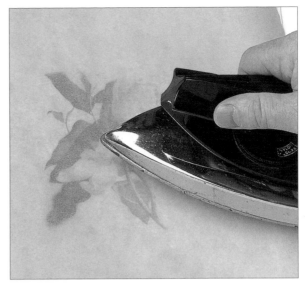

4. Iron the silk gently to dry it, using minimal pressure, or allow the silk to dry naturally.

5. Turn the silk over so the image is face up. Cover with a sheet of baking parchment and iron. Let it cool, then peel off the parchment.

Note

Once the image has been fixed, the silk can be washed gently in warm soapy water if required. When ironing the silk, always use baking parchment paper.

The finished design

The same simple technique was used to create the greetings card (also shown in the picture, right) which was designed by National Creative Workshops.

Cushions

The images used on the cushions, right, were taken from a collection of old photographs and postcards which belong to the designer, Robin Schoenfeld. It is always worth asking in antique shops and junk shops, as a surprising number of old family albums, letters and cards seem to end up there.

Floral quilt

Lazertran images are the central theme of this dyed cotton quilt made by Mary and Julia Sylvester. The reds and greens of the vibrant flowers are reflected in the warm colours of the surrounding patchwork pieces, and the effect is enhanced by the shaped edges of the quilt.

The method shown on pages 24 and 25 was used, with photographs of geraniums photocopied on to regular Lazertran and transferred on to white cotton. The rest of the cotton was dyed to complement the colours of the flowers and shapes were cut out of the fabric freehand using a rotary cutter. The quilt was machine stitched together to create a beautiful design awash with colour.

Polymer Clay

Lazertran Silk is used for this technique, which has been a great success with polymer clay artists. The method is quite simple, but there are a few tips to remember if you want to experiment.

   The clay should be flattened, softened and conditioned and any trapped air bubbles removed before the image is applied. One easy way to do this is by using a pasta machine. The clay should be also placed on a sheet of non-stick baking parchment while you are working, so it does not stick when the image is pressed on to its surface.

   The backing paper can be dampened with a brush, as shown in step 2 below, but you can also place the clay, with the image pressed on to it, in a bowl of water. If you swish the water gently, after a minute or two the backing paper will float off. This is better than trying to pull off the image, which sometimes results in tiny areas of the image being removed along with the paper.

   For this design, shells were photocopied on to a sheet of Lazertran Silk paper, which was then trimmed around the image.

You will need

Polymer clay
Non-stick baking parchment
Lazertran Silk
Brush or sponge
Craft knife
Cord

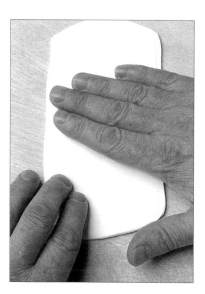

1. Prepare the clay by rolling and smoothing it. Apply the image to the surface, making sure the whole image is gently pressed on to the clay. Leave it for about 30 minutes, until the colours melt into the surface of the clay.

2. Wet the backing paper with a sponge or a brush and leave it to soak in for approximately two minutes. Alternatively, you can immerse the whole thing in a shallow tray of water and let it soak, swirling the water until the decal comes away.

3. Peel away the backing paper carefully, making sure that you do not pull away any small areas of the image.

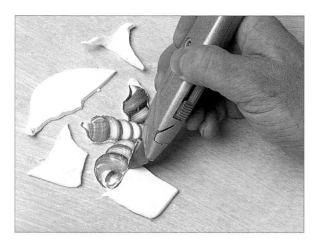

4. Cut round the image carefully using a craft knife, trimming as closely as possible to the contours of the design.

5. Make a hole in the top of one of the shells to take the necklace cord. Place the design on a baking sheet and bake it in a domestic oven, following the clay manufacturer's instructions.

Note

If bubbles appear on the image, just leave it for a few hours and they should disperse.

After baking the clay, some artists apply a coat of liquid polymer clay over the image and re-bake it. The surface can then be burnished to give it a glossy finish.

The finished design

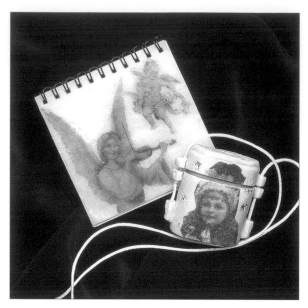

Festive notebook and box

These designs by Patty Barnes use polymer clay as a base. The notebook images were applied to translucent clay, with gold composition leaf sandwiched between the layers, and accented with pearlised powders. The same method was used on the little box.

Triptych

The centrepiece of this triptych by Robin Schoenfeld is a photograph of a celebrated and eccentric 19th-century beauty, the Countess Castiglione, who early on realised the artistic and popular impact of photography. She had a vast wardrobe, and was photographed wearing all kinds of costumes and in all kinds of poses. Here she is in the Queen of Hearts outfit she wore to a spectacular costume ball. The Empress of Germany reputedly remarked that one of the hearts was positioned quite inappropriately! The poor lady did not age well, and ended her days, penniless and quite mad, in Paris.

The central photograph was transferred on to translucent polymer clay with Lazertran Silk, and the other collage elements were selected to reflect the designer's impressions of the Countess' brilliant, though ultimately tragic, career. The triptych panels were painted bright red in honour of the Queen of Hearts.

Wood

As is the case with most surfaces, there are several ways to apply images to wood. If the wood is already varnished, applying a Lazertranned image is simple: acrylic medium or watered down craft glue can be used. Just follow the steps below.

If you are working with raw, untreated wood, you can still use acrylic medium or craft glue to apply the decals. In this case, it is best to seal the wood with one coat of acrylic medium, before photocopying and applying your images. Then follow the step-by-step instructions below.

Further images can be applied in the same way, and can even be laid on top of one another to give an unusual decoupage effect, in which you can see one transparent image through another (see pages 58-59).

If the wooden item you are decorating has awkward edges, curves or corners, use a hairdryer. The hot air will soften the applied images so that they stretch round or into difficult areas. Complete the job with a few coats of varnish; the decals are so thin that it will cover the edges and give a smooth finish.

You will need

Wooden object
Regular Lazertran
Acrylic medium or craft adhesive
Brush
Varnish
Tray of water
Scissors

1. Brush the surface of the wood, where you want the image to be placed, with acrylic medium.

2. Cut the image out and soak it in a tray of water for about two minutes. Remove the backing paper, then lay it down on the acrylic medium.

3. Using a brush, smooth away any excess acrylic medium, creases or air bubbles. Allow to dry.

Turpentine method

Remarkable effects can be achieved by applying images to untreated wood using real turpentine. Turpentine melts the decals and the images migrate into the wood, making them part of the surface. This method can be used even if the wood is an odd shape or is uneven in texture.

Photocopy the image, then cut it to size and soak it in water. Lift it out and blot away any excess water with absorbent paper, as water and turpentine do not mix. Next, paint the wood with turpentine and slide the decal off the backing paper, ready for laying on the treated surface. The best way to do this is to lift and drop the image into position, rather than sliding it, as the turpentine will start to melt the decal immediately.

When you are happy with the position of the image, paint on turpentine. Take care not to apply too much, as the design may start to break up. Do not worry too much about bubbles or even creases: these will melt out overnight. If any small bubbles or shiny areas remain the following day, a little more turpentine can be brushed on to start the process again.

Decorative wooden container

The main design is a photocopy of a lino-cut by Stuart Evans. The lid is decorated with a complementary computer-enhanced design by author Mick Kelly.

Wooden storage box

Interesting effects can be achieved using the turpentine method described on the previous page. For this decorative set of drawers, computer-enhanced images were photocopied on to regular Lazertran and applied directly to the untreated wood. Turpentine was then used to melt the transferred images, making them part of the surface of the wood.

Wax

Decorated candles can be a stunning addition to your decor. Regular Lazertran and Lazertran Silk can both be used.

Lazertran Silk

Art students have discovered the Lazertran Silk method of transferring images on to wax, while experimenting with the paper. It involves melting the wax and pouring it on to a sheet of Lazertran Silk images. It is allowed to set, then the wax is soaked in water, trapping the toners in the surface. This technique is extremely effective, but if you are tempted to try it, take care when heating the wax: molten wax can be extremely hot.

Regular Lazertran

The technique for transferring an image to a candle is simple yet extremely effective (see below). First, photocopy the image on to a sheet of regular Lazertran and cut it to the required size. Soak it in water until the image is released from the backing paper, then apply it to the candle.

You will need

Candle
Regular Lazertran
Scissors
Tray of water
Rubber squeegee

Note

If you would like your image to have a more polished appearance, warm it gently with a hairdryer, then dip it in heated wax. When the wax has set, it can be polished to a shiny finish.

1. Slide the image carefully from the backing paper on to the candle.

2. Smooth away any creases or air bubbles using a soft rubber squeegee.

The finished candles

Image reproduced by permission of the Tate Gallery, London.

Stone

To apply images to stone, use regular Lazertran. Choose stones that are light in colour as the applied colours will show up better. The best effect is achieved by melting the image into the surface with real turpentine, which should be used on any difficult, rough surface including pebbles, rocks and seashells. This project uses computer enhanced designs of insects on a group of stones.

Accuracy is not essential when you trim the image that is to be applied. The areas that show up as white behind the design are transparent when the backing paper falls away, and merge into the surface when they are applied. You do not need to press or force the image into any curves or hollows on the surface, as the transfer dissolves in the turpentine and sinks in. If there are areas where it has not sunk in properly after the piece has been left to dry second brushing with turpentine will restart the process and 'iron out' any problems.

You will need

A light-coloured stone
Regular Lazertran
Real turpentine
Shallow tray of water
Scissors
Absorbent paper
Soft brush

1. Cut around the transfer with scissors. Do not worry about leaving a white margin.

2. Soak the image in water. Pat off any excess moisture gently using absorbent paper.

3. Brush the top of the stone gently with turpentine, using an old paintbrush.

4. Position the cut-out image on the top of the stone, pulling away the backing paper at the same time.

5. Press the image into place gently with the brush. Apply another coat of turpentine immediately. Leave overnight.

Note

When using real turpentine, always heed the manufacturer's instructions. Protect your hands with gloves, and make sure you work in a well-ventilated room.

Do not touch the image once the final coat of turpentine has been applied, or it will break up.

The finished design

Goddess Hathor leading Queen Nerfertari

This image, which was designed and painted originally on glass by Julia Bottrell, was photocopied on to regular Lazertran paper, then applied to a textured stone surface using the turpentine method (see page 40). The original image has taken on the form and texture of the rugged surface, sinking into the natural curves of the stone. Turpentine was applied over the surface after the image was in position.

Metal

One of the simplest ways to use Lazertran is to apply it to metal, or any non-absorbent shiny surface such as ceramic or glass. There are two ways to do this depending on the type of finish you want. The most basic method is to use a design like the computer-enhanced image used here, photocopied on to Lazertran paper. The second method, which gives a water-resistant finish, is shown in the Ceramics section (see page 50).

When the image is in position, it can be fixed by simply letting it dry, then varnish can be applied to its surface to protect it. Another way to fix the image is to let it dry, then put it in a domestic oven on as low a setting as possible. Bake on the low temperature for 10 minutes, then increase the oven temperature gradually over a period of approximately one hour, until the transfer melts on to the surface. Take care, as if the oven is too hot the colours will gather in tiny balls, giving the transfer an antique look. As a rough guide, the final oven temperature should be about 350°F (180°C). The best indication is the way the object looks when baked: when it is ready to remove from the oven it will have a glazed appearance. Very shiny means it is ready!

You will need

Metal container
Regular Lazertran
Tray of water
Scissors
Squeegee
Varnish

Opposite
the finished canister

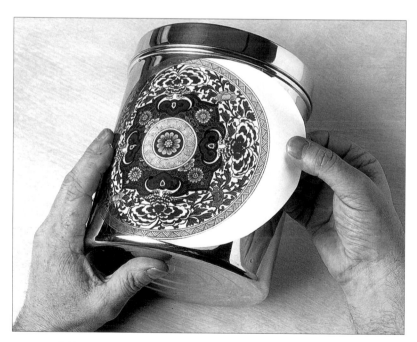

1. Carefully trim the image with scissors. Soak it in water for approximately two minutes then gently pull off the backing paper, while sliding the image on to the smooth surface of the canister.

2. Smooth away any creases or bubbles with a squeegee. Leave your work overnight to dry, to fix the image. If the item is to be handled often, apply a coat of protective varnish after it is dry, as the image will scratch easily.

Metal foil

Beautiful effects can be achieved easily if you transfer colourful or black and white images on to metal foil. There are many different types of foil, and these are available from most art and craft stores. It is worth experimenting with simple image applications or overlaying (see page 58). Lazertran Silk paper should be used and the image should be photocopied in reverse.

A sheet of pewter has been used in the demonstration below. This is particularly effective because the colours melt into the metal as the surface becomes hot. If you want to use pewter, take care not to let the iron touch the surface of the metal, as this will make it melt.

Once the image is has been transferred on to the foil surface, it can be embossed and folded. Make sure the tool you use is not too sharp, as you may scratch the image.

You will need

Pewter or metal foil
Lazertran Silk
Tray of water
Iron
Card blank
Photograph album

1. Place the design face down on to the foil. Using a hot iron, press the back of the paper until the design sticks to the surface of the foil.

2. While it is still hot, immerse the foil and Lazertran paper carefully in a shallow tray of water. The backing paper should float off.

3. Pull away the backing paper gently, remove the foil from the tray and let it dry. Reheat the foil to fix the colours by placing it on an upturned iron on a low heat setting.

Album and card

These original designs were created by Julie Hickey. A stencil embossing tool was used to emboss the images, then the same tool was used to hammer texture into the background. The designs were mounted on coloured card and used to decorate an album and a matching card.

Detail

This enlarged detail of the picture opposite shows the Lazertran image on metal foil. The background is beautifully embroidered, which enhances the smooth, golden areas of foil and complements the rich texture of the stitches.

Icon

This beautiful picture was made by Maggie Grey. The icon image,
taken from her sketchbook, was photocopied on to Lazertran and
then transferred on to metal foil. This was applied to a fabric made
by bonding tissue paper to iron-on interfacing. The whole piece
was machine embroidered with metallic and silk threads, creating a
gorgeous, rich surface for the central image.

Ceramics

Regular Lazertran is used to transfer designs on to smooth, glossy ceramic surfaces. There are two methods. The simplest can be used on tiled walls:

You will need

Ceramic tile
Regular Lazertran
Absorbent paper
Sponge
Bowl of water
Scalpel & metal rule
Squeegee

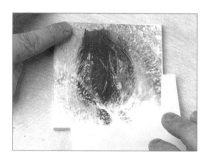

1. Photocopy the image, then cut it to size and soak it in clean warm water for two minutes, or until the transfer slides off the backing paper. Place the transfer on the tile and slide out the backing paper from under the image.

2. Smooth away any creases or air bubbles with a soft rubber squeegee and allow to dry. To protect the transfer, apply a coat of varnish over the whole surface. This will give the strongest finish.

The finished tile, decorated with an image by Ron Davies of Aberaeron.

Individual tiles

Loose tiles can be baked to give them a more durable waterproof finish. The process is for decoration rather than for tableware, so if it is used on ceramic plates or mugs, they should be washed by hand rather than in a dishwasher.

The image should be photocopied in reverse on to Lazertran paper, because it will be applied face down on the ceramic surface. Place the photocopied Lazertran in a domestic oven on a medium heat for a minute or so, or until the image becomes shiny. This will melt out any tiny air bubbles that may be trapped in the colours, avoiding pin-holes later. Follow steps 1 and 2 above, but this time apply the Lazertan face-down and slide off the backing paper. To dry out the transfer, place the tile in a domestic oven on the lowest possible setting, leaving the door open. After 10 minutes, close the door and leave it for a further 10 minutes. Over the next hour, gradually increase the oven temperature to around 180°C (350°F). The more slowly you do this the less chance there will be of the colours bubbling. When the image has a shiny finish it is ready. Leave it to cool.

Sail away

The strong, bold, dark colours are enhanced by the glossy white ceramic surface of the tiles. Experiment with other images. The techniques are simple and extremely effective.

From a lino-print by Stuart Evans.

Glass

There are a few points to remember when using Lazertran on glass or any transparent surface. A standard photocopy relies on the whiteness of the paper background to give body to the colours. Photocopiers do not use white ink, so any white areas of your image will show as clear on the finished design. The transfer is applied in the same way as for ceramics, using the same methods (see pages 50-51).

A stronger image can be achieved by applying two images, one on top of the other. This is not as difficult as it sounds and no special skill is needed to position and register the second image exactly on top of the first. This technique gives beautiful, rich colours when the light shines through the glass surface.

You will need

Lantern
Regular Lazertran
Absorbent paper
Sponge
Bowl of water
Craft knife
Squeegee

1. Photocopy the image, then trim off any excess paper carefully using a craft knife.

2. Soak it in water for about two minutes, then remove the backing paper and slide the image on to the glass panel of the lantern.

3. Remove any air bubbles or creases with a soft rubber squeegee.

Right
the finished lantern

Jewellery designed and made by Carol Heppner.

Glass jewellery

Images were stamped in black ink on to white paper, coloured with ink and coloured pencils and photocopied on to regular Lazertran. The glass shapes were cut out, secured with copper foil and soldered. Clear glue was used to secure the Lazertran images to the glass and glass paint to seal them.

Lamp

Computer enhanced images were photocopied on to regular Lazertran and applied to the lamp (opposite) using the techniques shown on pages 52 and 53.

Plate

Computer enhanced butterfly images were transferred on to the back of a glass plate (below). Smaller butterflies overlay larger ones in a circular dance, giving life and movement to the design. To complete the effect, the back of the plate was gilded.

Stamping and embossing

Stamping and embossing on to difficult surfaces like candles, curved surfaces, corners and awkward edges has been impossible up until now. With Lazertran, you can do just that – simply and easily! There are a few things to remember, but the techniques are uncomplicated and fun.

You should use waterproof stamping inks and stamp only on the glossy side of regular Lazertran paper. If you use embossing powders, first wipe the surface of the Lazertran paper with an anti-static cloth (the type of fabric that you clean spectacles with) so the powder does not cling to the shiny surface.

Scraps of Lazertran left over from other applications can be used, and you can stamp images over a previously-printed sheet to give fantastic effects. You can also use permanent markers to colour the Lazertran before or after the stamping and embossing process. After stamping, a hot air gun is used to dry the ink, or to set the embossing powder.

You will need

Lazertran paper
Stamps
Anti static cloth
Waterproof stamping ink
Embossing powder
Heat gun
Scissors

1. Wipe the glossy side of the Lazertran paper with an anti-static cloth.

2. Ink the stamp with black waterproof ink, then stamp the image carefully on the paper.

3. While the ink is still wet, sprinkle embossing powder on to the image.

4. Shake any excess powder back into its pot and heat the image with a heat gun.

5. Cut out the image and soak it in water for two minutes, then slide it off the backing sheet and position it on the candle. Remove air bubbles gently using a squeegee.

Note

Do not worry if the paper cockles while the image is being heated with the heat gun. This is normal and will not affect the image.

Stamp by Rubber Stampede

Overlaying

Beautiful effects can be achieved easily using this technique. As the Lazertran images are transparent, they can be overlaid, as in decoupage, one on top of the other. This allows the layers beneath to show through and can help to create wonderful, harmonious collages. If these layers are laid over painted or gilded surfaces they can look stunning. Images can also be applied to the back of a glass plate which has been coated with paint or metal leaf, to create unusual and effective designs.

The technique is simple. Photocopy the images and trim them, without worrying about accuracy as any areas which appear white will become transparent when the backing paper falls away. If the design runs over awkward edges or curves, hot air from a hairdryer will help to stretch it around corners.

When you are happy with the design, brush the overlapped images with decoupage varnish. The Lazertran transfers are extremely thin, so unlike regular decoupage, you will only need a few layers of varnish to create a smooth finish.

For this project, fern leaves and poppies were photocopied on to regular Lazertran paper.

You will need

Lazertran paper
Acrylic medium or craft adhesive
Brush
Varnish

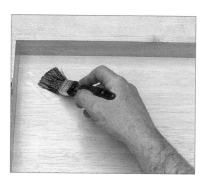

1. Prepare the surface by brushing a layer of adhesive over the area where the first image is to be placed.

2. Begin to overlay the images, pulling the backing paper away and smoothing away any creases or air bubbles.

3. Paste the surface carefully each time you apply another image. Build up the design gradually, until you have covered the whole area.

Opposite: the finished tray

Surface decoration

Lazertran Silk can be applied to almost any surface, including walls, floors, ceilings, furniture and even party balloons, using the method shown on these pages. It can be also used on fabric, as long at is not going to be washed very often, giving a slightly softer result than when you use regular Lazertran. For example, designs can be transferred when you are making a quilt (see page 28), or applying cross stitch and needlepoint designs to canvas.

Simply photocopy your chosen image in reverse, cut it out, then apply an even coat of spray mount. When this is tacky, place the image face-down on the fabric and iron it. Soak the backing paper off with a damp sponge and wipe away any gum. Finally, when the fabric is dry, place baking parchment over the image and iron it. When it is cool, remove the baking parchment.

This method can also be used if you are transferring designs on to paper and water is not appropriate, for example when you are working on a journal or memory album. Images on paper can also be fixed by ironing.

You will need

Lazertran Silk paper
Spray mount
Brush
Sponge

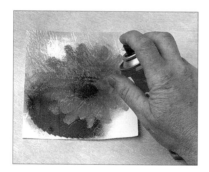

1. Cut out the image and spray it with spray mount. Leave it to become tacky.

2. Place the image face down on the surface. Press firmly rubbing the image well into the paper until it is secure.

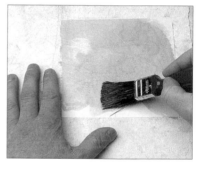

3. Brush the back of the image with water. Leave it to soak for two minutes.

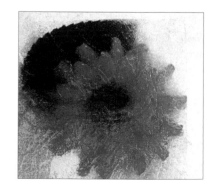

4. Carefully peel away the backing paper.

5. Gently sponge away any excess glue.

The finished picture
from a photograph by Ron Davies.

Conclusion

In this book we have shown a selection of the ways you can use Lazertran and Lazertran Silk transfer papers. Many current uses were developed in response to questions from art students looking for new ways of expressing themselves. We have also attracted a host of dedicated crafters who are discovering new ways to use Lazertran. Their enthusiasm and interest gives us the impetus to experiment and discover further ways to use these amazingly versatile papers. We are constantly searching for new techniques and applications.

In the time this book has taken to come to print there have been some interesting developments, especially in interior design. Friends in Japan are applying Lazertran images to baths and showers as well as other surfaces, and protecting these surfaces with industrial finishes.

Finally we would like to encourage you simply to have a go. With Lazertran, you can create totally individual pieces of craftwork or decoration for gifts, parties or home decorating. Be adventurous, be creative and most of all – have fun!

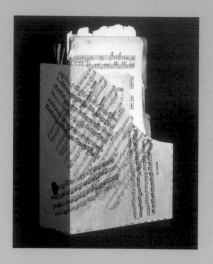

Musical notes were overlaid on a wooden surface to create an original decorative file, above. The same technique was used on the ceramic vase beneath. Leaf skeletons were colour photocopied, then single images were laid on the glossy surface and built up and overlaid to create an interesting pattern.

For the image, left, a photograph of a glass painting by Julia Bottrell was photocopied on to regular Lazertran, then transferred on to metal foil. The glowing background is a perfect complement to the colourful image.

Index